I0410003

Arcade Afterlife:

A Short Guide to Arcade Machines

Written by Ryan Albright

Introduction

This book is intended as a general guide to arcade machines and coin operated games. The information provided here is provided as is and is not intended as the final say on any subject that may be covered in this book. Using the information in this book is at your own risk.

Readers are encouraged to do there own research and use this book as it was intended. That intent being a GUIDE to coin operated machines and games.

In this book my aim is to teach you the general information you need to know in a plain simple way to do it that's strait to the point. There is no index for a reason. I want you to read it from cover to cover. There is a lot of information to read and its all important.

Chapter One: "Arcade History"

This is a difficult subject to tackle in chronological order. So this section is going to be broken up into smaller sub sections simply to help prevent confusion. The other reason is to prevent the authors head from exploding from trying to explain in perfect chronological order.

Arcade Games:

In no particular order lets start with arcade games. One word comes to the historians mind who study's arcade machines from the start to the finish. That machine being the one and only PONG.

Pong:

Pong was not the first arcade game to be released but it was the first arcade game among the original games to draw in massive crowds to play it. I know its hard to comprehend but people actually lined up to play this game back in the 60's before being replaced by more popular games like Berzerk and Asteroids.

Space Invaders:

The first game with scaling difficulty was Space Invaders. A truly unique game for its time. The ships going slow at first then when you get down to 1 ship the sudden speed increase was actually NOT intentional. What happened here was the ships on the screen as they get "destroyed" they released memory on the board and the ship suddenly moves faster. This is also why your tank moves faster as well.

There is a legend that this game was so immensely popular that it created a yen shortage in japan. The legend doesn't make a whole lot of sense from the grounds that the operators typically didn't stick the money in a old sock and bury it out behind there estates. They took the money back to there bank where they then deposited it. The money would of stayed in circulation and the likelihood this legend is true is very slim at best.

Donkey Kong :

Donkey Kong or DK is an arcade classic. You play as "Jump Man" who is trying to rescue his girlfriend named Pauline from Donkey Kong. Jump Man/Mario has to jump over barrels DK rolls down at him.

This game was a sensation when It was released by Nintendo and swept the market. Quickly followed by other games Donkey Kong 2 and junior. There was a Donkey Kong 3 But in the arcade it was released as a conversion kit and not a factory manufactured game.

There was also several illegal bootlegs made. Most notable was "Crazy Kong". For those of you not aware a bootleg is a unlicensed mod to a game. These are not very common, you can find them there just not common is all.

Should be noted that troubleshooting a bootleg can be a very serious thorn in the side. You can do it but expect a lot of trouble in doing it. Before buying any bootleg do your homework on it.

Pac-Man:

Pac-Man was released in 1980. The game was a highly grossing game that spawned spin offs and a lot of merchandise. The game generated over two billion dollars since the 80's.

For the one person who was thawed out in the year 2000 who has never heard of Pac-Man. The idea of the game is you run around a maze avoiding ghosts while trying to eat all the power pellets in the maze. Doing so will allow you to advance to the next level. If a ghost touches you pack man loses a life. Lose all your lives its game over.

The Pac-Man Character is possibly one of the most recognized video game characters ever. Falling just short of Jump Man/Mario.

Fortune Tellers:

Fortune tellers in the ""Penny Arcade"" years originally took just a penny and were typically of a "Gypsy Grandmother" design. The price was actually a decent amount of money back in the day. Various versions of these machines exist but all of them run off the same principle. Insert your money and hear a fortune be either told to you or you get your fortune on a piece of paper.

One of the earliest surviving examples is known to be in Virginia City. Estimated to be around 1 MILLION dollars. Known as a verbal fortune teller there is only 2 known to still exist today. The Virginia City fortune teller is unique because it was among the first machines that would speak its fortune to the listener.

The best known fortune teller to ever exist would be the "Zoltar" fortune teller. Seen in the movie "Big" this fortune teller became a major hit despite none actually existing at the time except for the prop in the movie. Today you can buy a Zoltar for about 6,000 - 8,000 at the time of my writing this book.

Pinball and Bagatelle:

Bagatelle games are the great grandfather of pinball in a sense. The game evolved out of the want for taking out door games of the late 15th century and getting them inside so they could be played even when the weather was bad. This ultimately over the years lead to variations of the games and served as the inspiration for other games such as the pachinko and the pinball machine.

Bagatelle games were generally played by setting up up pegs on the table and your goal was to get the ball into a hole in the bagatelle table while knocking over as few pegs as possible. Knocking over pegs counted as a penalty which would reduce your score. Eventually these pegs were actually fixed to the table and the game became more standardized.

The very first pinball machines were table top bar games much in the style of a bagatelle game. They evolved over time to take money were as the bagatelle game and some of the earliest games didn't take any money at all. These games were Pre-Flippers and were known as ""Wood Rails"".

A General Guideline of when the updates were made on pinball machines by year

- Somewhere between 1750 - 1775 - The Spring Launcher was invented

- 1931 Coin Acceptors were added to pinball machines

- 1933 Electricity, Solenoids, and General Illumination for the play field and back glass introduced.

- 1947 Flippers were introduced to help the player not drain the ball as fast. All machines before this were woodrails.

- 1970 with new technology came a major update for the pinball industry with a complete transition from "electro mechanical" to "solid state" and digital score displays. This change over also marks when circuit boards were first starting to be used in pinball machines.

- 2013 Jersey Jack Pinball Creates the first pinball machine to use a LCD screen for the back glass. Also the first time a major manufacture has used a actual computer to run a pinball machine

Mutoscopes

These machines were the precurser to movies. You'd put your nickle in, and a timer would start the motor. You'd watch the cards flip inside and the scene would play out. Although antiquted by todays standards the machines are still a unique snapshot of older arcades back in the 40's.

The Flip cards inside the machines were black and white. operation generally took about 1 minute to view the whole scene. Only one person could watch the reel at one time.

These machines are typically no longer manufactured. The pieces that exist command a premium in good condition. If you can find one with all of the cards still in it and the reel than it might be worth your while to pick it up.

Trade Stimulators

These machines were used typically by grocers. A lesser known fact is the fruit on the reels of slot machines were from the trade stimulators that were in grocery stores. If you matched three cherrys you won cherrys, so on and so forth.

During prohabition these countertop games would be used as dodges around the gambling laws of the time. The pay out would be along the lines of "win a pack of cigarettes!" which in the more unscrupulous shops you'd get paid the value of a cigarette under the table at these places.

These machines had no pay out's you always got paid under the table. There was all kinds of dodges the owners used to get around the gambling laws of the times. Everything from using tokens to sticking a gumball machine or a mint dispenser on the side and in some cases right inside the machine.

End of chapter fun fact - Machines that take money in exchange for a service have been around for century's. The earliest known vending machine was made by Hero of Alexandria, It dispensed holy water inside the temple and was a considerable source of income for the church

Chapter Two: "Why Older Machines Got Trashed"

Older games that were "routed" back in the 60's and sometimes even up to today were created with one intent in mind. That intent was to make as much money for the operator or owner as possible. The route operators typically only would do the minimum amount to keep a machine working.

Operators typically approached the owner of a high traffic area and made a deal with the owner to place the machine on there property in exchange for the owner making profit. This was generally lucrative for the owner but also caused the machines to get worn and torn even faster than normal.

Most operators were not repair professionals. This lead to a whole host of issues with why the machines were torn apart not just from game play but from improper maintenance as well. Unfortunately nice examples of older machines are harder to come by because of this fact.

The operators generally didn't or don't know how to replace or fix most of these parts. It's not an actual saying for them but they follow what I call "when in doubt throw it out" If they think it will take longer than its worth to repair it they will just throw it out and buy a new one. That is at least what they did in the past.

Chapter Three: "How To Negotiate A Purchase"

Sellers obviously want to make the most money they possibly can and as a buyer yours is to get as much money as you can for the purchase price. There is some things you need to know and keep in mind when your looking at any purchase. Those things will be described in detail below.

#1 Rule of buying, the seller usually isn't an expert. When your dealing with a seller who just has a casual interest in arcade machines and coin operated items. It's a safe bet that they usually do not know the actual retail price of the item.

This can work in your favor or against you. In your favor being the seller has the item too low for the condition of the machine. Not in your favor the seller has the price jacked up to the moon on its price and trying to talk them down can sometimes be an exercise in futility.

Most people go off the internet for there prices. The typical place everyone uses in 2014 is eBay. Unfortunately what ends up happening in this instance is when you get a whole bunch of people together who don't actually know the prices and start going off each other. Usually the price starts to go up until its unrealistic.

Suddenly a machine missing its back glass, it's missing pop bumpers, the GI lights don't light up, and the coin door is missing. What ends up happening in this hypothetical pinball machine situation is the price goes up to retail plus a large chunk of change. This happens because the seller went on eBay looked at the prices and said "well if those are that expensive then mine must be more expensive since mines in better condition!".

Chapter Four: "Understanding Condition VS The Price"

RESEARCH!!!! I know I don't have to shout at you but I cannot stress this point any harder if I tried. Well at least in print, if i was in the room your reading this in I'd probably grab you by your shirt and shake you shouting "RESEARCH!!!!!". Ok getting serious now why I keep shouting that is if you don't know anything about the machine and its none working you might end up paying too much for it.

Example Time:

Lets say you bought a Pac Man for $1,000 working. There is damage to the side art, and the control panel overlay needs replaced, and the bulb and marquee are missing. Your budget for repairs you set aside without having it planned out was 200.00.

The Side Art Costs You In Repairs - $126.00

The Control Panel Cost You To Replace - $65.00

Marquee Replacement - $30.00

Light Bulb - $8.00

Total Cost Of Repairs - $228.00

Over budget by $28.00

Twenty eight dollars isn't a huge amount of money but if your budget is tight it stings a little. Little numbers also add up over time and that's a polite example. Some machines don't have easy parts that people reproduce all the time. The Price goes up on replacement parts for those machines.

Obscure games or less favorable games parts are harder to find. The prices for replacement parts for less favorable parts are going to be way up there. NOS or new old stock items are going to be among the most expensive replacement parts anyone can buy.

Sometimes people do make reproduction parts. These parts can sometimes be cheaper, or they can actually be more expensive than NOS. Whatever the price is not everything needs to be replaced on these machines.

What most new buyers don't realize is that just because a part doesn't work doesn't necessarily mean you need to run to eBay or a online store and immediately buy a new part. Sometimes that is true but a good chunk of the time its not. You can salvage parts sometimes and spend a few penny's rather than spending a few dollars on brand new parts.

A good example of a common expense people don't understand they can easily fix in most cases is arcade buttons. Be it on a pinball machine or off a arcade game the buttons are actually incredibly simple to take apart and repair. Simply put take the button apart and put it into a plastic safe cleaning solution and the grime will come off.

Even disassembling it and running the parts under water can remove the dirt and grime from it. Every once in a while the spring needs replaced but that's a 20c fix in most cases. The money you save just cleaning parts will save you tons of money in the future.

Chapter Five: "Ok I'm Feeling Confident... Where Do I Find A Machine?"

Good question, and a simply complex answer. There is several places you can look for machines. The answer has variables though. Do you want it shipped to you, or are you willing to drive to get it, How much do you want to spend?

So you want it shipped to you?

This option is good but you have to wait for transit times. You usually have to deal with a third party shipping service, and theres the possiblity of damage when its not in your hands. The upside is other than being there when it shows up you pay a large chunk of money and just have to sit and wait for it to show up.

Most sellers on most sites expect you to deal with the shipping yourself. I am not going to cover it as I do not have experiance having machines shipped to me. The Idea is still an option though and should be seriously considered. Just make sure you ship a machine worth the money. Theres no sense in having a $100 machine shipped to you for $400 dollars.

Driving to go get it? Consider this:

Cost of gas is going up. If its a machine that is on one side of the contient and your on the other it might actually be more economical to have it shipped to you instead of going to get it yourself. Remember cost of gas is actually X2 if you go to get it. Driving there driving back, food, and if you need to stop at a hotel for the night thats more cost as well and remember a "good deal" that costs you more in gas to go get is not such a good deal.

How much are you willing to spend?

I am by no means saying you shouldn't travel to get your machines. What I am doing is pointing out the mistakes that a lot of new collectors make. They don't budget for repairs. They do not budget for travel expenses or take into consideration for possible damage to the machine from transportation of it themselves. Restoration takes A LOT of cash to do right.

There is multiple places to check for machines. If its listed below there is a good reason for it.

eBay

Ebay Is by far the most commonly searched site. However for shipping that is incredibly unlikely to have happen as most sellers on there demand you come and pick it up yourself. So if your like me and not a fan of driving this might not be the option for you. Some sellers will crate and ship but don't expect a professional job and expect to overpay on shipping.

Some sellers will allow you to arrange a third party to come crate and ship it to you. I can't vouch for that or the procedure of doing it but its an option to consider.

Etsy

Yes, the knitting captial of the internet. Why on earth is this on here as an option?! Theres a good reason, a lesser known fact is that if an item is over 10 years old Etsy considers it vintage.

On rare occasion you can find a great deal on etsy for coin operated devices SHIPPED to you. Again don't expect a professional shipping job but its still a good plan.

KLOV Forums

This option is possibly the single best option on here. The KLOV forums is the hub of most of the collectors online. It cost me a whopping 2 dollars to sign up on there forum so its worth the money and its a 1 time cost. There is good deals to be had here but everyone is a collector. A good deal does not last long. The plus side since everyone is a collector dealing with them is generally smoother than dealing with people in the next section....

Craigslist (DUN DUN DUN!!!!!)

Craigslist gets a bad wrap in the news. It's got its ups and downs depending on who your dealing with. If your dealing with local deals than this is your listing to deal with. Very hard to argue with "local" when were talking buying something. Just take a friend with you who you know has your back just in case because you never know. Do not carry cash, pay with a check. That way if your robbed its a lot harder to get money out of you. Be smart and you'll be fine.

Chapter Six: "Sizing Up The Seller"

Sellers typically are not money hungry monsters. Don't get me wrong sellers want to get as much money as they can but there still normally human. Sellers will budge but it takes some experience with haggling to make a seller come down on there prices.

Before going over the different types of people your going to encounter it's a good idea to learn some things first.

The 1st Thing - Make sure that when you talk to the person, you deal with the person in any way shape or form that you are absolutely nothing but professional, polite, and courteous. Remember bad attitudes and swearing even not at the person just like "@#$% dude that's a nice game!" might upset the seller and they might be less willing to deal with you.

The Second Thing - Sellers typically wheel and deal with people more if they have a common interest with the dealer. Look around the place the game is in find something you know about and comment on it.

Lets say in the game room the game is in there's a Firefly figure. Bring it up and get to talking about it. By you doing this the seller is lowering there guard. Also by having some common ground the seller gets to know you. Knowing you means there more willing to negotiate the deal down in your favor saving you money.

The Third Thing - DO NOT UNDER ANY CIRCUMSTANCES FIX THE MACHINE BEFORE PURCHASING IT! If you fix it there the seller will suddenly see dollar signs in his eyes. If the machine is a "none working for parts" machine and you go "all you need to do is plug the monitor in" then obviously the price is only going to go up since its an easy fix.

It seems more sleazy than it actually is. Your not doing anything wrong to buy the machine as none working and fix it yourself. Your making the seller room and putting money back in there pocket while getting a good deal. I would suggest that if its an easy fix and you know it that not haggling would be advised since your getting a discount anyways don't be getting greedy and blow the deal by trying to cut the price down further.

The fourth thing - NEVER set the price. Haggling is the act of getting the most for as little as possible. If you set the price too high the seller is going to snatch the price up.

-Example Time-

The seller is thinking $100.00 and says "What do you think its worth?". The inexperienced buyer will say something likely higher best case $200 or maybe higher not knowing the buyer could of been haggled down.

The experienced buyer would say "I don't know what price do you want to get out of it?" By phrasing it that way your getting the question back off you and back onto the seller. Getting them to say what there thinking allows you to have a bench mark and sets the highest price as your going to offer less if its too high or snatch it up if its a good enough deal your not even going to argue with there price.

Chapter Seven: "All Of The Strange People Your Going To Run Into"

Your going to find yourself meeting all kinds of people as well when your trying to free there machines from there homes or businesses.

The Dealer - The dealer is someone who knows what they have and what they are selling. Negotiating with this type of seller is extremely difficult. They usually know what they have and aren't willing to budge on there price much since they typically know if your not buying it someone else they know is and they will buy it.

The Clueless Person - The clueless person is the preferable person to deal with. Sometimes there just given a machine it works for a while when it breaks they just want to get rid of it, Or they get the machine from a relative. They have no intent on keeping it for themselves and again just want to be rid of it. Whatever there reason there willing to wheel and deal to be rid of it most times.

Sometimes there prices can be higher though because eBay again. They don't know better on the price. The good news is you can usually talk them down by pointing out just how much of a pain in the butt it is to fix a machine like this and how much money its going to take to restore it as well.

The Stubborn Seller - This is possibly the worst case scenario. This seller is possibly the hardest situation to come in and deal with.

Your facts may not matter they have a price in mind and by all that is holy they WILL not budge for ANYTHING. It doesn't matter to them there over priced, it can be a pile of ashen sludge and they'd still want 2k for it.

I don't recommend trying to haggle in this case. Assess the machine, if its worth the money buy it. If it's not worth the money pass on it you can always find a better deal later.

The Collector - The collector is a mix between "The Dealer" and possibly "The Stubborn guy". Sometimes the collector will put a machine up for sale due to pressure from there significant other or they supposedly need the money. In reality they don't want to part with it at all and the price is usually jacked up to the moon. Like with "The Stubborn Guy" they might not be very willing to haggle since they don't want to sell. I recommend with this type to try to get to know them. Figure them out, find common ground and use it as leverage to help negotiate a better deal.

And the last type

The "I'm Never Home" Guy - This type your lucky if you ever get in contact with them. They will set up times for deals but your in your car half way there when you get a call "yeaaaaa i forgot there's something I got to take care of today im gonna have to meet up with you next week".

Truthfully with this type your better off when they pull that put your foot down. If they keep doing this go "Now Look! I'm not going to keep wasting my time set a date and stick with it!" Failing that pass on the deal you'll probably never get it and use this only as a LAST resort.

Chapter Eight: "Condition! Condition! Condition!"

There is really nothing more important than knowing what condition the machine is in and what the cost of repairs of any given machine is going to be. I covered this lightly in another chapter but its absolutely important to research any given machine before buying it. Knowing how much you need the buyer to come down is absolutely paramount.

To know the condition though you must know what to look for on any given machine. Not only that but knowing the common failure points of the machines your buying is also extremely helpful as well when you go out and buy a none working machine. Knowing the common failure points means you can have a better idea whats wrong with any particular machine before you shell out money for a machine that might be a complete pain in the rump to restore.

The things to look for in a pinball machine in the wild:

- Check the plastics. Are they all there? If yes is there any damage?

- Check anywhere the ball enters the playfield and travels under the playfield for wear on the art around the entry ways.

- Speaking of art check the art for flaking, ware, and tare. If there is any present where is it. Is it in some barely noticeable place or is it in a major easy to see place on the play field. Can it be easily patched or is the art complicated?

- Is the backglass present? If so is there any flaking? If so how noticeable is it? The more noticeable the more the value goes down especially the older machines as there much harder to find NOS or reproductions.

- Does the machine power up without issue? If so does everything work properly? If not then the price should be negotiated down

- Is everything unlocked? The door, and back box? If not opening them isn't too difficult but again its a good negotiation point.

- The playfield glass has no cracks. This is important because on older machines, this can be costly to replace. Sometimes certain machines have special coatings on the playfield glass. A prime example is "Revenge From Mars" The top part of the playfield is coated in a special reflective coating.

EXTREMELY expensive to replace if broken and worth the time to check for.

- What is the condition of the cabinet? If the art is faded or damaged thats another strike against it. Especially check for bubbling around the legs with newer games. Sometimes the movement can ware around the leg protectors and sometimes it bubbles up.

- Is the playfield inserts bubbled? Sometimes the inserts where the lights are shrink due to age. This is repairable but it is a time consuming process and kind of a pain to do or a bit expensive to have replaced.

-

What to look for on an Arcade Machine

☐ Does the game power up?

☐ The marquee does it have flaking?

☐ The bezel is in good shape?

☐ No water damage to the cabinet?

☐ Is the cabinet warped?

☐ Minimal damage to the side art, control panel?

☐ If the game powers up do the buttons work?

☐ In most cases if the back panel is missing its not a huge issue, BUT in rare cases some of the back panels were supposed to have a concave bulge shape to allow for the monitor which can be a difficult challenge to replace. At best time consuming to replicate. Impossible to duplicate no, time consuming/costly yes.

I know this is a lot to keep in mind and look for. I truly understand where your coming from it took me a long time to learn it myself. I recommend researching more about restorations and what to look for. I also recommend following Rule #1 "do not fix the machine at the buyers location"

Chapter Nine: "So I Bought A Machine..... Now What?"

So.... you decided to jump into the waters of a restoration, or sometimes a resurrection is more accurate for some machines. Ok let me help you with some of the #1 most common problems found with most machines. These lists are not definitive but intended to help you get your bearings while you try to figure out whats wrong with your machine.

Knowing is half the battle with these machines, and sometimes its the simplest of things that your not thinking about that decides to be the wrench in your resurrection plans for the machine.

A brief list of things that were improperly done to most pinball machinesImproper

- valued fuses used to get the game "playable" but not actully fixing the issue.

- Coils being cleaned with the wrong type of cleaning solution that caused the coils to lock on and burn up.

- Batterys being left on the board. If they leaked they could damage the board.

Things typically wrong with Arcade machines

- Improper Valued Fuses / Blown Fuses

- Capacitors Dried Out

- Monitor Burn

- Missing/Damaged Maquees

- Damaged Side Art

- Water Damage

- Buttons/Joystics Being Gummed Up or Broken

Before you power on any machine you should always check the machine over mechanically first. Anything that isn't original needs to be checked because people don't always know what there doing when they work on a machine. They will tare a machine apart and rewire things that don't make sense in ways that'd make an engineers head explode.

Ok so you've gone through it and found the obvious problems. What you need to do is start going through is making a list of all of the problems. Once you have the list made the next step is to start figuring out where to start and in some machines that is a difficult decision to make.

The first place to start with a pinball machine is typically to remove the batterys if it has them remove them from the back box. For the new people reading this book who've never touched a arcade machine in there lives or seen one in person up till now. The batterys I am refering to are not the power supply in the machine.

On the head of the machine behind the back glass most older machines have a battery pack mounted right onto the board. The first thing to check here is that those batterys have not exploded. If they have exploded that's definately the first place to start because the batterys will eat a board to pieces. Ive heard if the damage isn't too terrible it is possible to use vineger to nuteralize the acid damaging the board.

Another good place to start is if you do power the pinball machine on and you smell a distinct burning smell power the machine off and start looking for a overly warm coil. Typically its the one with the blackened or distorted paper coil sleeve around it. It's either sticking on or theres a short in the power line going to that coil.

Either way your going to want to verify that the power going to it is correct and that the coil is not sticking on.

It is adviseable to clean all the coils before you start just so you know that all of them are clean and it removes failure points you have to check later. You see if there all clean and you personally did it right as in used the proper cleaning solution that doesn't attract dirt than you know later when one of them is getting hot that its a short. Its not a bad idea to clean all of the coils anyways since no one has probably cleaned them since the 80's.

If the back glass has flaking there is a way to prevent more of it from flaking off. I recommend before doing this to a 1,000 dollar back glass though practicing on a cheap one because you do NOT want to damage a 1,000+ dollar back glass with inexperiance. The method is you use triple thick on the backglass to help keep the remaining paint adheared to the glass.

You don't have to do that but it helps if you want to keep the machine as original as physically possible. The damage to the backglass is caused by the incandecent bulbs used before LEDS were invented. How Incandecent bulbs do the damage is that the heat from the bulbs is much hotter than an LED and it caused the paint to flake off. Triple thick can prevent the rest of it from coming off.

In Conclusion

This book is a guide to help you get started and to hopefully instill into you what I feel when I see an older machine. My knowledge is wasted where I'm living at the time of writing this book and in a way I'm hoping that my knowledge can truely help someone out there.

Part of me feels with the economic events going on in the US that we need more people who know how to restore items rather than just throw an item away and buy a new one. If this book helps even one person do that than I consider it a success.

If your looking for an Index by skipping to the end there is no index. Start from the cover and end at this **word**

www.ingramcontent.com/pod-product-compliance
Lightning Source LLC
Chambersburg PA
CBHW081808280526
45789CB00008B/3050